PROSPERITY 101™

Job Security through Business Prosperity™

by
Linda J. Hansen

contributing writers
Stephen Moore and Herman Cain

Special Thanks To:

Steve Moore
for his friendship, advice, and expert additions to this publication

Herman Cain
for his friendship, vision, and wise counsel

Mark Block
for his professional advice, support, and encouragement

Diane Slotman
for her invaluable assistance

Everett (deceased) & Frieda Cil.
for raising me with love

Jared, Dedra, Caleb, Jordan, Jenna, Jolynn
I am blessed to be your mother, which motivates me to
protect freedom for future generations

Zachary Kyle McDole, Jr. (Z.J.)
Your new life reminds us to stay vigilant

Additional Thanks To:
John Fund, David Mulcahy, Brenda Hicks, Don Hansen,
Gordon Gallagher, Rob McDonald and John Rovens.

1st Edition, 2009, 2nd Edition, 2011
Copyright © 2011 by Linda J. Hansen

Published by Prosperity 101, LLC
P.O. Box 510564
New Berlin, WI 53151
www.prosperity101.org
info@prosperity101.org
For additional copies, please send an email to the above address.
ISBN No: 978-0-9836986-0-9

Created by Linda J. Hansen
Graphic Design by Phil Landowski, Linda Hansen and Dimitri Lutsker

Additional Credits:
Section II "Policies for Prosperity" contains sections written by Stephen Moore and
Herman Cain and are used with permission.

This book is respectfully dedicated to the hard-working men and women who earnestly labor to provide for their families, save for the future, and pursue their American Dream. It is also dedicated to creative entrepreneurs and business leaders who work diligently, take risks, and shoulder the responsibility of providing jobs for millions of Americans.

It is also written with grateful appreciation to all Americans who have served in our Armed Forces. Thank you for risking your lives to protect our freedom and prosperity.

Job Security through Business Prosperity™

Prosper

pros'pėr. v.i. to thrive, to succeed; to turn out well –
v. t. to cause to thrive or succeed – n. prosperity, the
state of being prosperous: success, good fortune –
adj, prosperous, thriving, successful – adv.
prosperously. L. prosper, or prosperous, successful.

Introduction

Prosperity. Job security. You think about it, you worry about it, but what can you do about it? You go to work every day, giving your best efforts in hopes of keeping your job through every economic cycle and every corporate downsizing. You worry about the possibility of losing your job. Will you be included in the next round of layoffs? You wonder if you will be able to pay the bills, replace the aging vehicle, provide for a sick relative, or even have the luxury of a vacation.

Do you know your job security is not just dependent on your performance? Do you understand the economic influences that affect your employment and your ability to earn and save for the future? Are you aware of proactive steps, beyond excellent performance, that you can take to help secure your future employment and opportunities for advancement? Prosperity 101™ is designed to help you be educated and informed about issues that affect your employer, your job security, and ultimately, your family. Prosperity 101™ is designed to empower you: the employee, to go beyond your paradigms and look at job protection in a new way.

You may be surprised to learn about foundational principles that affect your life every day, and you may be even more surprised to learn how you can impact policymakers to improve the economic environment for your job, your family, and your country. I wish you all the best as you learn and earn. May you be prosperous!

I. Foundations of Prosperity

Prosperity. We all want it; we all work for it. We want to dream, create, achieve, and prosper. But how is prosperity created? How is it protected or destroyed? Why are some countries prosperous and some in a state of economic chaos? What conditions need to be in place in order for citizens to personally prosper? The answers may surprise you.

Our Founding Fathers came from a variety of economic, educational, and occupational backgrounds. However, their combined years of experience led to a collective wisdom that was innovative, revolutionary, and visionary. They envisioned a society that would offer economic freedom to all; a society that rewarded new ideas, hard work, and an entrepreneurial spirit of discovery and creativity. It was an experiment, but the experiment worked. The American Experiment was launched, and in just a few short years, America became a leader in the world economy.

It may seem surprising in our "everything-must-be-new" instant society, but our nation's founding documents provide a valuable road map to economic prosperity. The time-honored values of individual freedom, limited government, and free enterprise have served to guide the United States into economic prosperity and global leadership. We are the nation that people risk their lives to reach. We are the nation that offers opportunities to all, regardless of creed or color. The values embodied in our founding documents and the liberties they create inspire people to swim across oceans to reach our shores and proudly cry with their hands on their hearts when Old Glory is raised.

Every American can benefit from understanding the founding principles that made our nation great. Our documents of freedom are easily accessible, easily understood, and timeless in their relevance to our daily lives.

Included in the appendix of this book are copies of The Declaration of Independence, the United States Constitution and The Bill of Rights. Study them; learn from them; apply them to your life. You will be glad you did.

The American's Creed

by William Tyler Page

I believe in the United States of America as a government of the people, by the people, for the people; whose just powers are derived from the consent of the governed, a democracy in a republic, a sovereign Nation of many sovereign States; a perfect union, one and inseparable; established upon those principles of freedom, equality, justice, and humanity for which American patriots sacrificed their lives and fortunes.

I therefore believe it is my duty to my country to love it, to support its Constitution, to obey its laws, to respect its flag, and to defend it against all enemies.

Written 1917.
Accepted by the United States House of Representatives on April 3, 1918.

II. Policies for Prosperity

The founding documents provide foundations for prosperity, but what are the policies that lead to a nation's economic prosperity, and subsequently to corporate and individual prosperity? The answers may surprise you.

People often tell us that government should provide for citizens by guaranteeing accessibility to a variety of goods and services which were previously obtained through hard work and determination. While all would agree that eliminating poverty, hunger, homelessness, or illiteracy are worthwhile goals, to imply that government is not the source to cure those ills often brings accusations of heartlessness and insensitivity. However, what does government have that it can give you? Many people do not realize that the government has nothing. I repeat; the government has nothing. It can provide nothing for anyone unless it takes it from someone first. It cannot give you something (a benefit or service) unless it takes something (taxes) from you or someone else first. Once your money is taken from you (in taxes), you no longer have control over what is done with it. Whatever you get back (in a benefit, service, or tax return) will be much less than you originally gave, due to the cost of administering those dollars.

Government can never create prosperity. It can only create conditions in which people and organizations can be prosperous. It is not the role of government to create prosperity; it is the role of government to allow prosperity. If we examine the visionary wisdom of our founding fathers, we can see that it is not the government, but private businesses and individuals that are truly the driving force in a solid and prosperous economy.

The remainder of this section is written by two very noteworthy individuals; Stephen Moore, senior economic writer at the Wall Street Journal, and Herman Cain, nationally recognized business leader and former radio talk show host. Cain's comments will provide a basis for understanding prosperity and economics. Moore's expertise and wisdom will simplify difficult concepts and help you to view the study of economics in a new light. You will be informed and encouraged as you read their selections.

Economics & the Basics of Prosperity

by Herman Cain

"Prosperity" is not a dirty word. Our founding fathers had prosperity in mind when they founded this country on the principles of life, liberty, and the pursuit of happiness. They believed every man, woman, and child should have an opportunity to pursue their dream - the American dream. Prosperity is exactly what was intended when this great country was founded.

This section will include a basic explanation about profit and economics and will include candid truths about national, corporate, and personal prosperity. Let's start with the basics:

What is Profit?
Profit is the difference between production cost and retail price. Put simply, it is the difference between the cost to produce an item and the final selling price.

Profit margin is your profit dollars expressed as a percentage of your retail price. Let's look at an example:

Retail price of Product A	$100.00
Cost to produce Product A	$90.00
Profit	$10.00
Profit Margin %	$10/$100 = 10%

Let's say you are entrepreneurial enough to hold costs down to $75.00 in the above example, or to sell Product A for $115.00. Your profit would jump to $25.00 and your profit margin to 25%.

Different businesses have different levels of profit and different levels of profit margins. Some businesses make more profit and some make less.

Why Must a Business Make a Profit?
When a business does not make a profit it is broke – it is without any money. If a company is broke it will eventually be bankrupt and/or it will shut down and close. Broke, bankrupt, or non-operating businesses cannot create jobs, hire people, or maintain positions for current employees.

Businesses that do not make money (profit) do not pay taxes. Businesses that do make money (profit) are responsible for all of the taxes collected by the government. Thus, businesses making a profit additionally provide money to the government for essential government functions. Whether you look at it from the point of the worker or the government, making a profit is a good thing. Making more profit is a better thing.

What Limits Profit?
Remember our earlier example on profit margin? Anything that increases the cost of producing a product, or decreases the price someone would pay for a product, makes profit smaller.

Taxation, regulation, and legislation can all have this effect on businesses and make it more difficult for a business to make a profit. Burdensome taxation, regulation, and legislation will, in the end, negatively affect you and me. They make profits smaller, and smaller profits mean fewer jobs and less tax revenue collected by the government.

What is the Free Market System?
Our economy is based on the simple principle of supply and demand - businesses will make only what the market wants and sell it only at a price the market can bear - with as little government interference as possible. America has the greatest economy in the world because of the free market system. However, our system is gradually changing to include more regulation and taxation by government, and that is not good for business.

If you look back at our history, people exercising their free will in a free market system is what made this country great. But it is under attack by too much legislation, regulation, and taxation. This has been increasing over decades, but today it is out of control. We must work to get it back under control where we have limited government and limited taxes to protect our prosperity for today and tomorrow. This is necessary to ensure our children and grandchildren can achieve their American dream.

What Can You Do?
There are three things you can do to protect your personal prosperity. First, you can become *informed* about threats to your prosperity. Reading this book is a great first step, but go beyond to keep yourself informed so you are better educated when you vote. Second, be *involved*. Register to vote and make sure you vote in every election. You can help guard against threats to prosperity with your vote. You can also be involved by becoming connected to an organization that reflects your values and helps to express your views. Last, but not least, be *impactful*. Voting makes an impact, but also be ready to protect your right to prosperity with your voice. Your voice and your votes are the two major weapons you can use to make sure we get this nation back on track.

What Is Your Responsibility?
My father left the farm at the age of eighteen, with just the clothes on his back and the dream to give his own children a little bit better start in life. He did provide us with better opportunities - thanks to his hard work, his free will, and the free market system that enabled him to chase his American dream. This is probably a very similar story to the dream your parents had and perhaps it is your dream.

He believed, as I do, that this is the greatest country in the world because of free men with free will and free markets   but we have to keep it that way. It is our responsibility not only to us, but also to our children and grandchildren and all the future citizens of this great country.

"When people have the right information, they will make the right decisions."

–Thomas Jefferson

The Keys to Prosperity

By Stephen Moore

Let's start with the premise that real and sustainable economic growth is generated by businesses incentivized to compete and discover the most efficient ways to provide goods and services for which there is a market. Government subsidies only distort that process. It is not pro-business or pro-growth to give special hand outs to one industry or another. We are against corporate welfare in all its forms.

The keys to prosperity are simple and timeless: low taxes, a lean and efficient budget that doesn't waste money or provide unwarranted subsidies, and low regulation.

Ronald Reagan understood this formula better than any president in recent history. The tax cuts that took place under the Reagan administration were largely inspired by his experience as an actor. Reagan explained that actors in his day would only make three movies a year. If they made a fourth, their tax rate would go up to such a point that it would be unprofitable. Reagan knew that the same logic applied to other sectors of the economy and in August of 1981, he signed into law the largest tax cut in history. He also reined in inflation with Paul Volker at the helm of the Federal Reserve and moved swiftly to lift many burdensome regulations. This was the beginning of the greatest period of prosperity in the history of the world. Between 1981 and today, more wealth was created than in the prior 200 years combined.

The policy works for Republicans and Democrats. John F. Kennedy's supply side tax cuts in 1961 serve as a shining example of good policy overcoming partisanship. President Kennedy knew that high tax rates were restricting growth so much that the federal government could increase revenue by cutting taxes:

It is increasingly clear that no matter what party is in power, so long as our national security needs keep rising, an economy hampered by restrictive tax rates will never produce enough revenues to balance our budget just as it will never produce enough jobs or enough profits... In short, it is a paradoxical truth that tax rates are too high today and tax revenues are too low and the soundest way to raise the revenues in the long run is to cut the rates now.

We wish politicians of both parties would take that advice to heart.

Telling the Story

The charts and figures on the subsequent pages are meant to give you an inside look at how the economic policy impacts the financial outlook. This section discusses how economic policy changes in the past 20 years have affected the markets and how changes in the years ahead influence the financial scene in the U.S and abroad over the next decade. It supports the belief of job security through business prosperity and points the way that we need to move as a nation.

The Keys to Prosperity

High inflation undermines growth. When you adjust the stock market for inflation, it's easy to see that inflationary periods had only artificial growth.

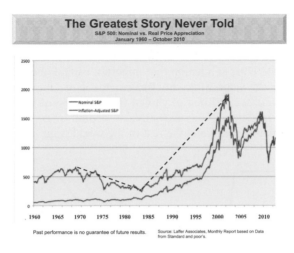

The Greatest Story Never Told
S&P 500: Nominal vs. Real Price Appreciation
January 1960 – October 2010

Past performance is no guarantee of future results.   Source: Laffer Associates, Monthly Report based on Data from Standard and poor's.

Tax Cuts Attract Capital

The figure below confirms that President Kennedy was right. When tax rates have fallen at the federal level the share of taxes paid by the wealthy has increased. In 1980 when the top tax rate was 70% the richest 1% paid a little less than 20% of all the federal income taxes. By 2007 when the top tax rate was 35%, or half what it was in 1980, the share of taxes paid by the wealthy actually rose to 41%. The best way to soak the rich is to cut tax rates.

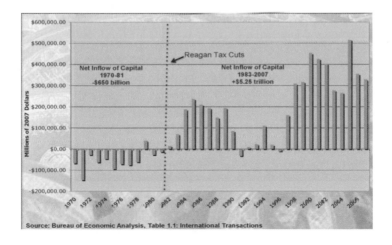

Source: Bureau of Economic Analysis, Table 1.1: International Transactions

Share the Wealth?

Tax cuts increase the incentive to work and invest. This is especially true when the potential rewards are greater. As marginal tax rates came down, the incentive to invest in the United States increased. We see in the figure below that the U.S. went from a nation that was exporting capital in the 1970s, to a nation that imported capital once the tax rates fell. In the 25 years after the Reagan tax cuts, the United States imported a net $5.25 trillion of capital from the rest of the world. The same is true in states. When tax rates fall, capital owners and business leaders from other states and the rest of the world want to invest in that state.

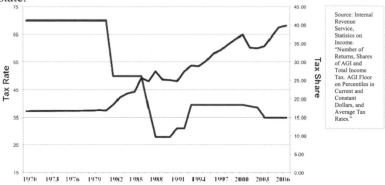

Bottom 95% Pay Less than Top 1%

There is a lot of talk in Washington and state capitals about how to promote equity and tax fairness. This figure below shows that the rich do pay their fair share in federal taxes. The top one percent of earners now pays a larger share of federal income taxes than the bottom 95%. Some critics argue that the rich pay most of the taxes because they make most of the income.

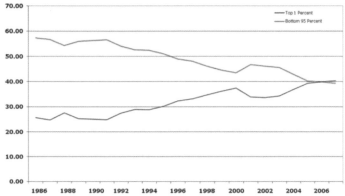

Rich Pay More Than Their Fair Share

It is true that the top 1% make about 25% of the income. But they pay an even larger share of the federal income tax. What is also worth noting is that the bottom 50% of Americans now pay only 3% of the total income tax. We already have a highly progressive tax system. Raising tax rates may cause the rich to pay a smaller share of taxes – just the opposite of what is intended.

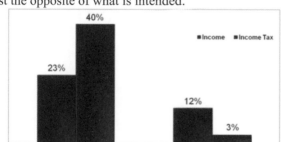

Source: Internal Revenue Service, Statisics on Income. "Number of Returns, Shares of AGI and Total Income Tax. AGI Floor on Percentiles in Current and Constant Dollars, and Average Tax Rates."

The Laffer Curve

The explanation for why lower tax rates lead to greater tax payments by the rich is captured by the Laffer Curve. Dr. Art Laffer's legendary napkin sketch, the "Laffer Curve," started a pro-growth revolution. When tax rates are too high, they prohibit growth and decrease the incentive to work, save, and invest. Decreasing marginal tax rates increases these incentives and, by growing the economy, can also increase revenue. This curve shows there are two tax rates that produce a certain level of revenues. This is because at a 100% tax rate, no one works and so no revenues are produced for the government. This means that sometimes tax rates are so high they lose revenues for the government. That can be true on the federal and state levels. We don't advocate the tax rate that produces the most revenues, but rather the rate that produces the most growth, which is often well below the revenue maximizing rate. And for states, the growth maximizing income tax rate…is zero.

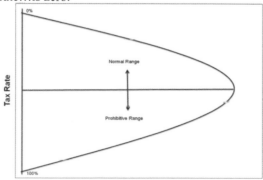

Tax Revenue

The Laffer Curve: Revenues vs Taxes

The often maligned Bush tax cuts created jobs at a near-record pace. Over the 2003 to 2007 period the U.S. produced 8 million new jobs. The reduction in tax rates on employers and investors incentivized job creation and businesses responded. Raising tax rates would slow the pace of new jobs. State and Federal Government should be concentrating on cutting tax rates, not raising them. After the Bush tax cuts, employment soared. Unfortunately, many of these gains have been wiped away by the financial crisis. Another supply side stimulus is what is needed to get employment back on track.

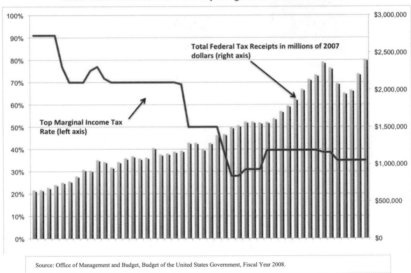

Real Federal Revenues and the Top Marginal Income Tax Rate

Source: Office of Management and Budget, Budget of the United States Government, Fiscal Year 2008.

Inflation Rate: 1950 to 2010

One result of high inflation is high interest rates. States are major borrowers, so high interest rates inflate the costs of state budgets. We worry that as monetary policy has loosened, the threat of more inflation and higher interest rates looms in the future.

Consumer Price Index For All Urban Consumers: All Items Less Food & Energy (CPILFENS)

Source: Bureau of Labor Statistics, Consumer Price Index, Available at: http://www.bls.gov/data/#prices

Show Me The Money?

This chart shows the monetary base – the amount of money circulating in the economy. If not reined in, this increase in the monetary base could turn into high inflation. As Milton Friedman taught us, inflation is too many dollars chasing too few goods. The Federal policy of printing money to create jobs hasn't worked very well to bring down unemployment.

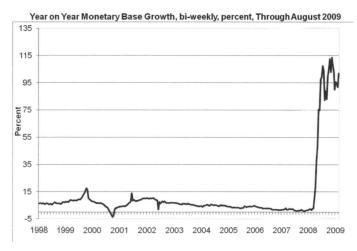

Year on Year Monetary Base Growth, bi-weekly, percent, Through August 2009

10 Year Treasury Note Yield

Investors have lost confidence in the Federal Government as a profitable place to lend money.

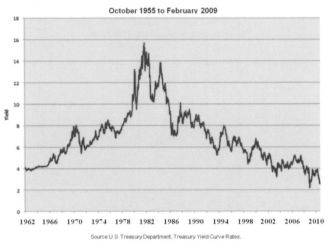

October 1955 to February 2009

Source: U.S. Treasury Department, Treasury Yield Curve Rates.

Education and Medical Prices Skyrocket
While Import Prices Drop

Two industries that are largely provided by government, particularly state government, are education and health care. These are two industries that have had nearly the highest rates of inflation over the past decade. We believe one reason for this is the third party payer system. A third party pays for health care – insurers or government – and for education – the government or scholarship programs. This immunizes the patient or family from the cost of education and health care. Subsidies for health care and education would be best if they were reduced, and better if the money were given to parents or worker directly, through vouchers or other means. Since health care and education are two of the largest items in state budgets, governors and legislators will have a difficult time balancing their budgets without reforms in these programs. The chart also documents the benefit of trade – whether among states or between countries. Many consumer items have fallen in price over the past decade – especially those items that are directly impacted by trade. Imports lower prices to consumers, thus stretching their paychecks and increasing their real standard of living.

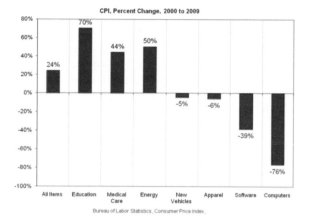

CPI, Percent Change, 2000 to 2009

Bureau of Labor Statistics, Consumer Price Index.

Worker Well-Being

An often repeated myth of the U.S. economy is that when taxes have come down only the rich have benefited while the middle class and poor have fallen further behind. The reality is that the middle class has made significant economic strides forward over the past three decades when tax rates started falling. Salaries for U.S. workers have risen about 20%. Counting fringe benefits, the average worker today earns about one-third more than a middle class worker in the 1970s. But looking at total consumption, we see that the average worker consumes about 50% more than his counterpart back in the 1960s or 1970s. The hallmark of the U.S. economy over the past several decades has been upward economic mobility. People have moved to higher income classes over time, though some have fallen. The U.S. needs to remain an opportunity society where people can rise and fall on their hard work, entrepreneurship, and talent

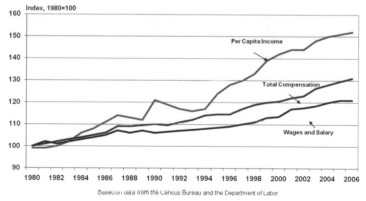

Based on data from the Census Bureau and the Department of Labor

33

The Ever-Improving American Dream

This chart tells the real story about America's middle class. The middle class is making more money today than in the 1950s, 60s, or 70s. Those considered middle class (making up the middle quintile of American families) has increased from those making between $33,408 and $44,800 in 1967 to those making between $45,021 and $68,304 in 2005 (in inflation adjusted terms). The middle class isn't shrinking; it is getting richer, though families suffered losses in income during the 2008-09 recession that could take years from which to recover.

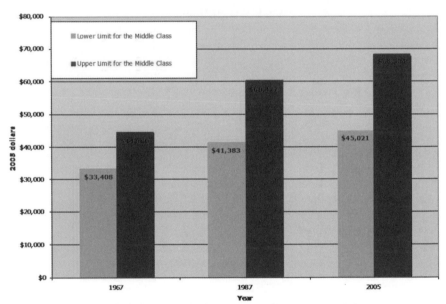

Upper and Lower Income Limits for Middle Class Families

Household Income, Available at: http://www.census.gov/hhes/www/income/index.html

Guns and Butter: Discretionary Spending Explodes

Now we turn to the bad news: the exploding federal budget. This is a lesson in what states should not do to get their economies growing faster. We can see that the budget was fairly constrained in the 1990s when Bill Clinton was in office and the Republicans controlled Congress. The budget was balanced as a result of expenditure controls and strong economic growth that generated massive revenues for the federal government and the states. But over the past decade both parties went on a spending binge unprecedented in America.

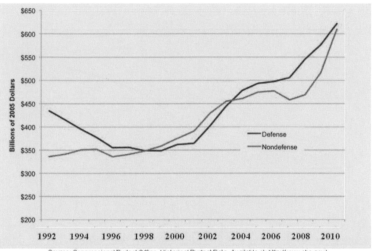

Source: Congressional Budget Office, Historical Budget Data, Available at: http://www.cbo.gov/

The Coming Tax Increase

President Obama and the Congress extended the Bush tax cuts for another two years in December of 2010. But they are still scheduled to rise again after 2012, and that would be catastrophic for the U.S. economy. This figure shows that taxes as a share of GDP would rise to an all-time high if that happens. The more money Washington takes from taxpayers, the harder it gets for states to balance their budgets, since federal taxpayers are also state taxpayers. We believe that one of the greatest dangers to the economy is that tax rates will be allowed to rise after 2012. This figure shows which taxes would go up, and by how much. These are taxes on workers, employers, and investors. The dividend tax would nearly triple from 15% to 43%.

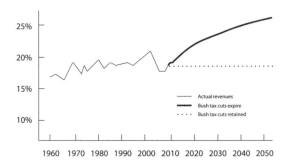

Hog Wild Spending

Barack Obama inherited a $500 billion deficit and through his spending policies allowed that budget to reach $1.3 trillion. It is not a pretty picture.

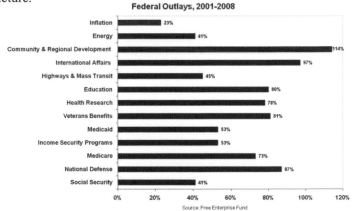

Federal Outlays, 2001-2008

Source: Free Enterprise Fund

Payroll Employment Fully Recovered

Inflation is a jobs killer. We see that in the 1970s when the economy was in the tank, the inflation rate skyrocketed. At one point the inflation rate hit 14% under President Jimmy Carter. These high inflation rates didn't help states; they caused costs to rise for all the things that states buy. State deficits rose as inflation rose. States should not be advocates of high inflation, but rather stable currency policies.

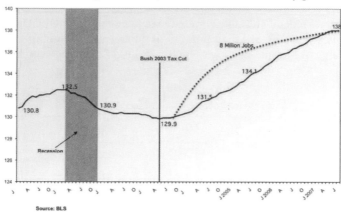

Source: BLS

The World Really is Flat

The last couple of decades have seen the rest of the world beginning to understand the virtues of supply-side economics, while the U.S. has been retreating. Many countries formerly beholden to socialism now embrace tax systems that are far more pro-growth than the U.S. system.

Isn't it time for a flat tax in America? This chart shows that many countries around the world have been adopting flat taxes. (By the way, Georgia and Jersey are the nations, not the states!) A flat tax of 15 to 20% would bring investment and jobs to the United States like a giant high-voltage magnet. It would also simplify the tax code and reduce special interest loopholes that lobbyists have carved out for their clients.

There is one area where the U.S. tax system has become particularly uncompetitive. That is our corporate tax applied to businesses. The U.S. now ranks second highest in the world when including state business tax rates. The chart below shows that the trend is unfavorable to the U.S. In the 1980s and early 1990s the U.S. had a corporate tax rate below the average of our competitors. Now we are significantly higher than the rest of the world – by an average of about 15 percentage points. Even Sweden has a lower corporate tax rate than the U.S. average and most of the 50 states. Almost everyone, including the Obama administration's own tax reform commission, believes this is putting the U.S. at a competitive disadvantage and costing America jobs. States with very high corporate tax rates, including California, New York, Iowa, and Illinois are at or close to having the highest combined federal and state corporate tax rate among all OECD nations. This is a sure way to export jobs out of these states and out of the U.S., entirely. We would put a very high priority on reducing state business taxes.

Flat Tax Nations and Their Rates			
Albania	10	Kyrgyzstan	10
Bulgaria	10	Latvia	25
Czech Republic	15	Lithuania	27
Estonia	21	Macedonia	10
Georgia	12	Mauritius	15
Guernsey	20	Montenegro	15
Hong Kong	15	Mongolia	10
Iceland	35.7	Prednestrovie	10
Iraq	15	Slovakia	19
Jamaica	25	Romania	16
Jersey	20	Russia	13
Kazakhstan	10	Ukraine	15

Source: Center for Freedom and Prosperity

Free Countries are Wealthier and Healthier

What the chart below is telling us is that nations which adhere closest to the principles of economic freedom, as measured by the Cato Institute, have had the most success in raising the living standards of their citizens. We have consistently found the same principle to be true for states. We as Americans, by virtue of the fact that we live in a country that is mostly free (though moving in the wrong direction in areas like health care), have a living standard that is roughly ten times higher than that of those who live in countries that repress the free market and don't respect individual rights. Additionally, some critics say that free markets, although they create growth, cause other problems, such as social inequities, pollution, and other injustices. We decided to look at another measure of well-being: health, as measured by life expectancy. What we found was that economic freedom is also highly correlated with a higher living standard. Free countries like the U.S. have nearly twenty years longer life expectancy than socialized nations with no respect for private property. This means that economically free countries are not just wealthier, they are healthier. Other studies have also found that economic freedom is also highly correlated with reductions in pollution levels. Freedom, low taxes, and prosperity are the best medicines to whatever is ailing a state.

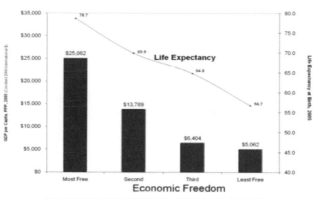

Source: Cato Institute and Fraser Institute, Economic Freedom of the World, 2007.

Future Threats to Prosperity

Politicians in Washington talk about an infrastructure deficit or a shortage of dollars for other public programs. But as the next figure shows, the federal budget has been on a stampeding path of growth for the past decade. Most programs have grown three or four times the rate of inflation. It is time for tight lids on federal spending and to return to 2007 levels of outlays to get the federal deficit under control.

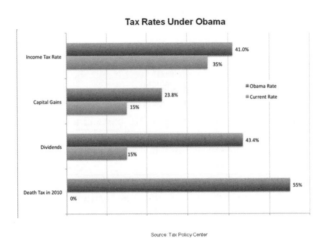

Source: Tax Policy Center

High Corporate Taxes Make the U.S. Uncompetitive

What policies are the best for promoting growth? The figure below explains succinctly. The policy ideas that lead to prosperity are those that are consistent with promoting economic freedom. This is true of nations and states. Economic freedom is defined as property rights, low taxes, light regulation, free trade, sound money, right of contract, private operation of business, and other such measures that limit undue government interference in the marketplace. In general, interferences with the free market inhibit growth.

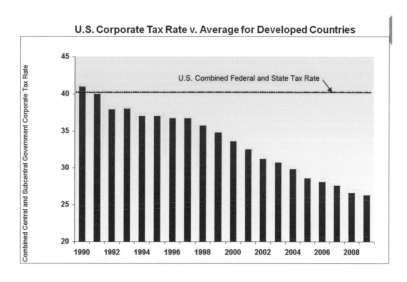

U.S. Corporate Tax Rate v. Average for Developed Countries

III. Protecting Your Prosperity

As you have seen from the previous sections, there are definite foundations and policies that affect our national prosperity, and in turn, corporate and personal prosperity. The link between what happens legislatively or judicially at state and national levels and what happens to your net worth is one that few people understand. Did you know you can have a large impact on public policy, and that by choosing to be proactive and informed, you can influence policymakers in many ways? Remember, our government was formed to be of the people, by the people, and for the people...NOT just by and for those who are in control of policy decisions. Never forget that elected officials are in position to represent YOU, not themselves or special interests, but YOU; the taxpayer and citizen. Hold them accountable by becoming engaged in the political process. It is not difficult and will take only a few minutes of your time. The results will be worth every bit of effort.

As a rule, if an elected official receives a phone call or letter from a constituent, they realize that at least one hundred others hold the same view. Taking just a few minutes out of your day to contact your elected officials about important issues can send a powerful message. Your phone call, letter, or email carries the influence of one-hundred people! Often, it takes the diligence of only a few people to influence a vote on an issue. Educate yourself and voice your opinion on issues that are important to you. And, if the elected officials do not listen to the voice of the people, we have the incredible freedom in America to replace them through the election process.

It is important to support those who will stand firm to support free market, limited government principles. It is equally as important to remove from office those who do not vote in accordance with our Constitution and in a way that represents their constituents honestly and responsibly. Ideas have consequences, and it matters who is elected. An uneducated vote is a wasted vote. Make your vote matter!

BECOME

✓Informed
✓Involved
✓Impactful™

Three Steps to Protect Your Prosperity

INFORM yourself on the issues and proactively seek out information regarding policies that will affect your job and your family. There are many resources which can help you. Join organizations that promote free-market, limited government principles and sign up for newsletters or emails from a variety of freedom promoting organizations. Tune in to radio or TV shows that inform you about current events and tax policies. Study. Compare. Investigate. Learn.

It is also important to become familiar with your elected officials and to understand their opinions on free-market issues. You will find a wealth of information through Project Vote Smart, a non-partisan resource for information about elected officials and candidates. Visit *www.votesmart.org* to learn more. If you are unsure as to who your elected officials are or how to contact them, please visit these websites to easily locate that information.

www.votesmart.org
www.usa.gov
www.nwyc.com

INVOLVE yourself in your community by engaging in activities which can promote the principles and policies that are important to your family and your company. Visit the websites listed above to gain ideas and information about organizations and events of interest to you. Attend candidate forums and town hall meetings, conduct research on the internet, and compare voting records of candidates. Start a book club, a neighborhood group, or a letter writing campaign. Volunteer! Do not sit back and wait for someone else to make a difference. YOU are the one who needs to act to protect your prosperity. The responsibility rests on your shoulders. Do not depend on others to do what you must do for yourself.

IMPACT society by being an educated and informed voter. Your vote DOES make a difference! Many elections have been won or lost by one vote. Make yours count by educating yourself and knowing who you want to vote for - and why - when you enter the voting booth. Make sure you are voting for someone who believes in the policies and principles that are important to you and to the security of your economic future. It is the responsibility of all Americans to participate in the electoral process. Many people sacrificed their lives and livelihoods for the freedoms we take for granted. Do not let their sacrifices be in vain. **Exercise your right to vote!**

Are you registered to vote?
Registering to vote is a simple process. If you are a United States citizen over the age of 18, you are eligible to vote. You may obtain voter registration information by contacting your local County Clerk. You may also find voter registration forms and information by visiting this website: **www.eac.gov** (A sample form is included in this publication.)

Simple Steps to Impact Elected Officials

As stated in *Protecting Your Prosperity*, there are simple things you can do to make an impact on public policy at the state and federal levels. Protecting your economic future is your responsibility. You may be very responsible about budgeting, saving, and planning for the future. However, if you do not INFORM and INVOLVE yourself to make an IMPACT on public policy, your efforts may be in vain. Higher tax rates, increased regulations, and a bloated government all contribute to fewer employment opportunities and fewer dollars in your pocket. Be an advocate for your economic future!

10 Tips for Contacting Your Elected Officials

Be Informed. Your credibility is vital. Be fair and well-informed.
Be Respectful. You may disagree, but do so respectfully.
Be Factual. Use key facts to add validity to your statements.
Be Original. Explain how this issue affects you personally.
Be Focused. Keep to one issue per letter, phone call, or visit.
Be Thorough. Include all information for informed decision-making.
Be Brief. Keep to the point and do not needlessly elaborate.
Be Persistent. It may take more than one contact to help them understand.
Be Grateful. Thank them for their time and consideration.
Be Thoughtful. Treat them as you would like to be treated.

A sample letter to an elected official follows in the appendix.

IV. Summary

As you have learned in the previous sections, free enterprise policies are what made this country strong and opened wide the doors of opportunity for people from all backgrounds and abilities to live out the American Dream. Taking a stand to protect economic freedom helps not only yourself, but your children and grandchildren. If you want your children to have the same or better opportunities than you have, then you MUST be involved to protect those liberties. Freedom is not free, nor should it be taken for granted.

INFORM yourself on the issues.
INVOLVE yourself in the community to promote the policies which will help you and your employer to prosper financially.
IMPACT society by being an educated and informed voter.

Job security only comes through business prosperity. Business prosperity can only be achieved through free market, free enterprise policies.

America offers the liberty that people yearn for and will risk their lives to experience. The longing for freedom is a universal fire that rages in the heart of man, and America sparks the flame that burns brightly across the world. You can help that flame of freedom grow to illuminate future generations.

The time is now. Do not wait to be involved. Act now to protect the security of your job, the prosperity of your family, and the freedom of your country. It is up to you.

"What is freedom? It is the sum total of all our freedoms. To be free, on one's own responsibility, to think and to act, to speak and to write, to labor and to exchange, to teach and to learn – this alone is to be free."

Frederic Bastiat (1801-1850)

Appendix

	SAMPLE VOTER REGISTRATION APPLICATION			○ Submitted by Mail *(Official Use Only)*
	Confidential Elector ID# *(HAVA - required if)* *(Official Use Only)*		SVRS ID	

1
○ New WI Voter
○ Name Change
○ WI Address

Municipality ○ Town ○ Village ○ City

County

2
WI Driver License or WI DOT-issued ID **(DL # required if issued)** | Expiration Date | ○ I have neither a WI Driver License/ID, nor a Social Security Number.

Social Security Number - Last Four Digits (if driver license not issued or not current and valid) | X X X - X X -

Current

Print your name exactly as it appears on the document, the number of which you provided in Box 2. *(Driver License/ID Card or Social Security Card)*

3
Last Name | First
Middle Name | Suffix (e.g. Jr, II, etc.) | Phone #
Date of Birth (M/D/YYYY) | Email Address

4
Residence Address: Street Number & Name
Apt. | City | State & ZIP

If applicable

5
Mailing Address: Street Number & Name
Apt. Number | City | State & ZIP

Previous Required

6
Last Name | First
Middle Name | Suffix (e.g. II, II, etc.)

7
Previous Registration Address : Street Number & Name
Apt. | City | State & ZIP

8
Accommodation needed at poll location (e.g. wheelchair access):

○ I am interested in being a poll worker.

If you do not have a street number or address, use the map to show where you live.
- Mark crossroads
- 'X' where you live
- Use dots for landmarks

9
Please answer the following questions by filling in "Yes" or "No":
1. Are you a citizen of the United States of America? ○ Yes ○ No
2. Will you be 18 years of age or older on or before election day? ○ Yes ○ No
If you filled in "No" in response to EITHER of these questions, do not complete this form.

10
I hereby certify, to the best of my knowledge, that I am a qualified elector, a U.S. citizen, at least 18 years old or will be at least 18 years old at the time of the next election, having resided at the above residential address for at least 28 consecutive days immediately preceding this election, with no present intent to move. I am not currently serving a sentence including probation or parole for a felony conviction, and not otherwise disqualified from voting. I certify that all statements on this form are true and correct. If I have provided false information I may be subject to fine or imprisonment under State and Federal laws. **If completed on Election Day**: I further certify that I have not voted in this election.
Please sign below to acknowledge that you have read and understand the above.

11
Signature of Elector | X | Today's Date (M/D/YYYY)
Election Day Voter # *(Official use only)*

Falsification of information on this form is punishable under Wisconsin law as a Class I felony. | Proof of Residence type *(official use only)*

12
Assistant Signature: | Assistant Address: | Proof of Residence # *(official use only)*

Official's Signature: | SRDs printed name and SRD#:

Ward	Sch. Dist.	Alder	Cty. Supr.	Ct. of App.	Assembly	St. Senate	Congress

GAB-131 (REV 6/2011)

53

SAMPLE VOTER REGISTRATION APPLICATION INSTRUCTIONS

These documents constitute proof of residence if they: **Contain the voter's current and complete first and last name and residential address, and are valid on the day used to register to vote.**	• A current and valid WI Driver License / ID Card • Any other official identification card or license issued by a Wisconsin governmental body or unit • An employee ID card with a photograph, but not a business card • A real property tax bill or receipt for the current year or the year preceding the date of the election • A residential lease (Does not count as proof of residence if elector submits form by mail) • A picture ID from a university, college or technical college coupled with a fee receipt • A picture ID from a university, college or technical college coupled with an on-campus housing listing provided by the university, college or technical college to the municipality that denotes US Citizenship • A utility bill for the period commencing not earlier than 90 days before the day registration is made • A bank statement • A paycheck • A check or other document issued by a unit of government
1	• Fill in the circle (New Voter, Name Change, Address Change) describing why you are completing this form. • A "New Voter" is anyone who is not currently registered to vote in Wisconsin. You can check your voter registration status at Wisconsin's Voter Public Access website (https://vpa.wi.gov). • Indicate your municipality. Use formal names (For example: City of Plymouth, Village of Chenequa, or Town of Aztalan). • Indicate your county of residence.
2	• If you have been issued and have a current and valid WI driver license or WI DOT-issued identification card (ID), you must provide the number. • If you have been issued a WI Driver License, which is revoked, suspended, or expired, please provide the number and the last 4 digits of your Social Security number. • If you have not been issued a WI driver license or a WI DOT-issued ID, you must provide the last 4 digits of your Social Security number. • If you do not have a WI driver license, a WI DOT-issued ID or a Social Security number, indicate that fact by filling in the appropriate circle. • If you are registering to vote on Election Day and have been issued a WI driver license, but are unable or unwilling to provide the number, your vote will not be counted unless you provide the number to the election inspectors by 8:00 p.m. on Election Day or to your municipal clerk by 4:00 p.m. the Friday following Election Day.
3	• Provide your current and complete name as it appears on the document, the number of which you provided in Box 2, including your last name, first name, middle name or initial and suffix (Jr, Sr, etc), if any. • Provide your month, day and year of birth. Remember to use your birth year, not the current year. • Providing your phone number and/or email address is optional, but will help your municipal clerk to contact you in case of problems with your registration, and is subject to open records requests.
4	• Provide your home address (legal voting residence), which must be located in Wisconsin. • Record the full house number (including fractions, if any). • Provide your full street name, including the type (St, Ave, etc) and any pre- and/or post-directional (N, S, etc.). • Provide the city name and zip that appears on mail delivered to your home address. • <u>You may not enter a PO Box as a residential address.</u> A rural route box without a number should not be used.
5	• If your mailing address is different from your home address, provide it here. A PO Box is acceptable as a mailing address. Overseas electors should provide their complete overseas address here.
6	• Provide your previous first, last and middle names, along with a suffix, if any. • Provide this information regardless of the time elapsed since your last name change.
7	• Provide your address where you were previously registered to vote. • Provide this information whether you moved within Wisconsin or from another state regardless of time elapsed.
8	• If you need assistance when voting, you may describe the assistance required (e.g. wheelchair access). • If you are interested in being a poll worker for your municipality, you may fill in the circle. • If you do not have a street address, use the map to show where you live.
9	• Answer both questions by filling in the appropriate circle. If you answer "No" to either question, you are not eligible to vote in Wisconsin. • Please note, for question 2, you must either be at least 18 years old, or will be at least 18 years old at the time of the next election to be eligible to vote. If you are completing on election day you must be 18 years old today.
10	• Please read carefully. By signing this form you are certifying that you meet the eligibility requirements to vote. If you do not meet these requirements, you are not eligible to vote in Wisconsin, and should not sign this form.
11	• By signing and dating this form, you certify that all the information you have provided on this form is true and correct, and that you meet the eligibility requirements for voting, listed in the statement in Box 10 of this form. • Falsification of information on this form is punishable under Wisconsin law as a Class I felony.
12	• **Assistant:** If you are unable to sign this form due to a physical disability, you may have an assistant do so on your behalf. That assistant must provide his or her signature and address in the space provided. By signing, the assistant certifies that he or she signed the form at your request.

GAB-131 (REV 6/2011)

Contact An Elected Official
Suggested Template

Date

To Your Senator:
The Honorable (full name)
(Room #) (Name) Senate Office Building
United States Senate
Washington, DC 20510
Dear Senator:

To Your Representative:
The Honorable (full name)
(Room #) (Name) House Office Building
United States House of Representatives Washington, DC 20515
Dear Representative:

Your letter should address a single topic or issue. Typed, one-page letters or emails are best. Many recommend a three-paragraph letter structured like this:

1. State who you are and your reason for writing. List your credentials.
2. Provide details. Be factual not emotional. Provide specific rather than general information about how the topic affects you and others. If a certain bill is involved, cite the correct title or number whenever possible.
3. Close by requesting the action you want taken: a vote for or against a bill, or change in general policy.
4. If you want a response, you must include your name and address, even when using email.

The best letters are courteous and to the point, and include specific supporting examples. Ensure that you identify yourself and contact information.

Sincerely,

Add Name/Address

HOW A BILL BECOMES A LAW

Thousands of bills are introduced in Congress each year, but not all become law. Thanks to the wisdom of our Founding Fathers, there is a plan in place to provide checks and balances for our lawmakers as they go through the process of introducing and voting on new legislation. This diagram shows a bill traveling through the House of Representatives and the Senate at the same time. This can happen, but often a bill is passed by one legislative body and then sent to the other for action.

Once a bill has been passed in both legislative bodies, it is then sent to the President, who can approve it or reject (veto) it. If the President vetoes a bill, it may still become law, but only if two thirds of the House and the Senate vote to override the veto. As you can see, there are several steps that must be taken for a proposed bill to become a law.

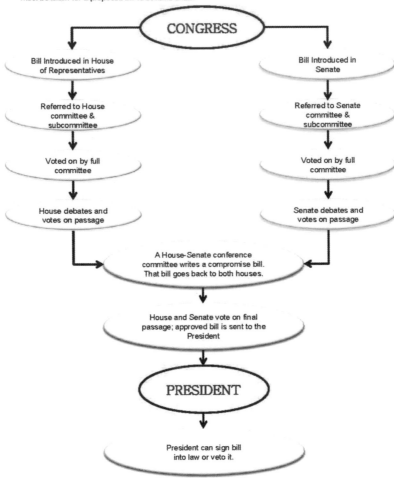

The United States government is composed of three branches: the Executive, the Legislative, and the Judicial. They are represented by the President, Congress, and the United States Supreme Court. Each branch plays an important role in governing.

The Three Branches of Government

The Legislative Branch
- Consists of the Senate, the House of Representatives, and various administrative agencies
- Makes, Repeals, and Amends Federal Laws

The Executive Branch
- Consists of the Executive Office of the President, the President's Cabinet, and the Corresponding Independent Agencies
- Conducts Administration of the National Government, Enforces Federal Laws, and Regulates Government Agencies

The Judicial Branch
- Consists of the Supreme Court (the highest court in the land), Federal District Courts, and Federal Courts of Appeals
- Handles cases that involve the U.S. Constitution and Federal Laws

Note: Each state is governed by three branches of government, dealing only with issues at the state level. For specific information about your state government, please visit this website provided through the Library of Congress: **www.loc.gov/rr/news/stategov/stategov.html**

Terms & Definitions

The Economy - A way to manage resources (good and services).

Gross Domestic Product - The value of resources (goods and services) produced in a country during a specific year.

Economic Growth - A positive change in production of resources (goods and services).

Job Creation Growth - A net increase in the number of NEW jobs in a given economy.

Unemployment Rate - The number of unemployed persons as a percentage of the total labor forces.

Trade Deficits - Imported resources (goods and services) exceed exported resources.

Exchange Rate for U.S. Dollar - A ratio of the U.S. dollar's value in comparison to the value of foreign currencies. In other words, the number of dollars needed to buy one unit of a foreign currency.

Federal Budget Deficit - Occurs when the national government spends more resources than it collects. Measured both Annually- the budget deficit totals measured for that specific year and Total- each annual deficit added together to comprise an overall federal deficit of a nation.

Unfunded Liabilities - A legally bound debt which is not backed by an asset of equal or greater value.

Global economy - A system of resource (goods and services) management that is made up of all national economies and expressed as a single system.

National Economy - A country's system of resource (goods and services) management which usually includes preference of that nation's resources over others.
State Economy- A state's system of resource (goods and services) management which usually includes preference of that state's resources over others.

Local Economy - A small area's system of resource (goods and services) management which usually includes preference of that area's resources over others.

Personal Economy - An individual's or family's system of resource (goods and services) management.

The Declaration of Independence

In Congress, July 4, 1776
The unanimous Declaration of the thirteen united States of America

When in the Course of human events it becomes necessary for one people to dissolve the political bands which have connected them with another and to assume among the powers of the earth, the separate and equal station to which the Laws of Nature and of Nature's God entitle them, a decent respect to the opinions of mankind requires that they should declare the causes which impel them to the separation.

We hold these truths to be self-evident, that all men are created equal, that they are endowed by their Creator with certain unalienable Rights that among these are Life, Liberty and the pursuit of Happiness. --That to secure these rights, Governments are instituted among Men, deriving their just powers from the consent of the governed, --That whenever any Form of Government becomes destructive of these ends, it is the Right of the People to alter or to abolish it, and to institute new Government, laying its foundation on such principles and organizing its powers in such form, as to them shall seem most likely to effect their Safety and Happiness. Prudence, indeed, will dictate that Governments long established should not be changed for light and transient causes; and accordingly all experience hath shewn that mankind are more disposed to suffer, while evils are sufferable than to right themselves by abolishing the forms to which they are accustomed. But when a long train of abuses and usurpations, pursuing invariably the same Object evinces a design to reduce them under absolute Despotism, it is their right, it is their duty, to throw off such Government, and to provide new Guards for their future security. --Such has been the patient sufferance of these Colonies; and such is now the necessity which constrains them to alter their former Systems of Government. The history of the present King of Great Britain is a history of repeated injuries and usurpations, all having in direct object the establishment of an absolute Tyranny over these States. To prove this, let Facts be submitted to a candid world.

He has refused his Assent to Laws, the most wholesome and necessary for the public good.

He has forbidden his Governors to pass Laws of immediate and pressing importance, unless suspended in their operation till his Assent should be obtained; and when so suspended, he has utterly neglected to attend to them.

He has refused to pass other Laws for the accommodation of large districts of people, unless those people would relinquish the right of Representation in the Legislature, a right inestimable to them and formidable to tyrants only.

He has called together legislative bodies at places unusual, uncomfortable, and distant from the depository of their Public Records, for the sole purpose of fatiguing them into compliance with his measures.

He has dissolved Representative Houses repeatedly, for opposing with manly firmness his invasions on the rights of the people.

He has refused for a long time, after such dissolutions, to cause others to be elected, whereby the Legislative Powers, incapable of Annihilation, have returned to the People at large for their exercise; the State remaining in the mean time exposed to all the dangers of invasion from without, and convulsions within.

He has endeavored to prevent the population of these States; for that purpose obstructing the Laws for Naturalization of Foreigners; refusing to pass others to encourage their migrations hither, and raising the conditions of new Appropriations of Lands.

He has obstructed the Administration of Justice by refusing his Assent to Laws for establishing Judiciary Powers.

He has made Judges dependent on his Will alone for the tenure of their offices, and the amount of payment of their salaries.

He has erected a multitude of New Offices, and sent hither swarms of Officers to harass our people and eat out their substance.

He has kept among us, in times of peace, Standing Armies without the Consent of our legislatures.

He has affected to render the Military independent of and superior to the Civil Power.

He has combined with others to subject us to a jurisdiction foreign to our constitution, and unacknowledged by our laws; giving his Assent to their Acts of pretended Legislation:

For quartering large bodies of armed troops among us:

For protecting them, by a mock Trial from punishment for any Murders which they should commit on the Inhabitants of these States:

For cutting off our Trade with all parts of the world:

For imposing Taxes on us without our Consent:

For depriving us in many cases, of the benefit of Trial by Jury:

For transporting us beyond Seas to be tried for pretended offences:

For abolishing the free System of English Laws in a neighbouring Province, establishing therein an Arbitrary government, and enlarging its Boundaries so as to render it at once an example and fit instrument for introducing the same absolute rule into these Colonies:

For taking away our Charters, abolishing our most valuable Laws and altering fundamentally the Forms of our Governments:

For suspending our own Legislatures, and declaring themselves invested with power to legislate for us in all cases whatsoever.

He has abdicated Government here, by declaring us out of his Protection and waging War against us.

He has plundered our seas, ravaged our Coasts burnt our towns, and destroyed the lives of our people.

He is at this time transporting large Armies of foreign Mercenaries to complete the works of death, desolation, and tyranny, already begun with circumstances of Cruelty; amp & Perfidy scarcely paralleled in the most barbarous ages, and totally unworthy the Head of a civilized nation.

He has constrained our fellow Citizens taken Captive on the high Seas to bear Arms against their Country, to become the executioners of their friends and Brethren, or to fall themselves by their Hands.

He has excited domestic insurrections amongst us, and has endeavoured to bring on the inhabitants of our frontiers, the merciless Indian Savages whose known rule of warfare is an undistinguished destruction of all ages, sexes and conditions.

In every stage of these Oppressions We have Petitioned for Redress in the most humble terms: Our repeated Petitions have been answered only by repeated injury. A Prince, whose character is thus marked by every act which may define a Tyrant, is unfit to be the ruler of a free people.

Nor have we been wanting in attentions to our British brethren. We have warned them from time to time of attempts by their legislature to extend an unwarrantable jurisdiction over us. We have reminded them of the circumstances of our emigration and settlement here. We have appealed to their native justice and magnanimity, and we have conjured them by the ties of our common kindred. To disavow these usurpations, which would inevitably interrupt our connections and correspondence. They too have been deaf to the voice of justice and of consanguinity. We must, therefore, acquiesce in the necessity, which denounces our Separation, and hold them, as we hold the rest of mankind, Enemies in War, in Peace Friends.

We, therefore, the Representatives of the United States of America, in General Congress, Assembled, appealing to the Supreme Judge of the world for the rectitude of our intentions, do, in the Name, and by Authority of the good People of these Colonies, solemnly publish and declare, That these United Colonies are, and of Right ought to be Free and Independent States, that they are Absolved from all Allegiance to the British Crown, and that all political connection between them and the State of Great Britain, is and ought to be totally dissolved; and that as Free and Independent States, they have full Power to levy War, conclude Peace contract Alliances, establish Commerce, and to do all other Acts and Things which Independent States may of right do. --And for the support of this Declaration, with a firm reliance on the protection of Divine Providence, we mutually pledge to each other our Lives, our Fortunes and our sacred Honor.

Signed by Order and in Behalf of the congress,

JOHN HANCOCK, President

Attest,

CHARLES Thomson, Secretary

Constitution of the United States

We the people of the United States, in order to form a more perfect union, establish justice, insure domestic tranquility, provide for the common defense, promote the general welfare, and secure the blessings of liberty to ourselves and our posterity, do ordain and establish this Constitution for the United States of America.

Article I

Section 1. All legislative powers herein granted shall be vested in a Congress of the United States, which shall consist of a Senate and House of Representatives.

Section 2. The House of Representatives shall be composed of members chosen every second year by the people of the several states, and the electors in each state shall have the qualifications requisite for electors of the most numerous branch of the state legislature.

No person shall be a Representative who shall not have attained to the age of twenty five years, and been seven years a citizen of the United States, and who shall not, when elected, be an inhabitant of that state in which he shall be chosen.

{Representatives and direct taxes shall be apportioned among the several states which may be included within this union, according to their respective numbers, which shall be determined by adding to the whole number of free persons, including those bound to service for a term of years, and excluding Indians not taxed, three fifths of all other Persons.[1]} The actual Enumeration shall be made within three years after the first meeting of the Congress of the United States, and within every subsequent term of ten years, in such manner as they shall by law direct. The number of Representatives shall not exceed one for every thirty thousand, but each state shall have at least one Representative; and until such enumeration shall be made, the state of New Hampshire shall be entitled to choose three, Massachusetts eight, Rhode Island and Providence Plantations one, Connecticut five, New York six, New Jersey four, Pennsylvania eight, Delaware one, Maryland six, Virginia ten, North Carolina five, South Carolina five, and Georgia three.

When vacancies happen in the Representation from any state, the executive authority thereof shall issue writs of election to fill such vacancies.

The House of Representatives shall choose their speaker and other officers; and shall have the sole power of impeachment.

Section 3. The Senate of the United States shall be composed of two Senators from each state, **{chosen by the legislature thereof, for six years; and each Senator shall have one vote.[2]}**

{Immediately after they shall be assembled in consequence of the first election, they shall be divided as equally as may be into three classes. The seats of the Senators of the first class shall be vacated at the expiration of the second year, of the second class at the expiration of the fourth year, and the third class at the expiration of the

sixth year, so that one third may be chosen every second year; and if vacancies happen by resignation, or otherwise, during the recess of the legislature of any state, the executive thereof may make temporary appointments until the next meeting of the legislature, which shall then fill such vacancies[3]}.

No person shall be a Senator who shall not have attained to the age of thirty years, and been nine years a citizen of the United States and who shall not, when elected, be an inhabitant of that state for which he shall be chosen.

The Vice President of the United States shall be President of the Senate, but shall have no vote, unless they be equally divided.
The Senate shall choose their other officers, and also a President pro tempore, in the absence of the Vice President, or when he shall exercise the office of President of the United States.

The Senate shall have the sole power to try all impeachments. When sitting for that purpose, they shall be on oath or affirmation. When the President of the United States is tried, the Chief Justice shall preside: And no person shall be convicted without the concurrence of two thirds of the members present.

Judgment in cases of impeachment shall not extend further than to removal from office, and disqualification to hold and enjoy any office of honor, trust or profit under the United States: but the party convicted shall nevertheless be liable and subject to indictment, trial, judgment and punishment, according to law.

Section 4. The times, places and manner of holding elections for Senators and Representatives, shall be prescribed in each state by the legislature thereof; but the Congress may at any time by law make or alter such regulations, except as to the places of choosing Senators.

The Congress shall assemble at least once in every year, and such meeting shall **{be on the first Monday in December,[4]}** unless they shall by law appoint a different day.

Section 5. Each House shall be the judge of the elections, returns and qualifications of its own members, and a majority of each shall constitute a quorum to do business; but a smaller number may adjourn from day to day, and may be authorized to compel the attendance of absent members, in such manner, and under such penalties as each House may provide.

Each House may determine the rules of its proceedings, punish its members for disorderly behavior, and, with the concurrence of two thirds, expel a member.

Each House shall keep a journal of its proceedings, and from time to time publish the same, excepting such parts as may in their judgment require secrecy; and the yeas and nays of the members of either House on any question shall, at the desire of one fifth of those present, be entered on the journal.

Constitution of the United States continued...

Neither House, during the session of Congress, shall, without the consent of the other, adjourn for more than three days, nor to any other place than that in which the two Houses shall be sitting.

Section 6. The Senators and Representatives shall receive a compensation for their services, to be ascertained by law, and paid out of the treasury of the United States. They shall in all cases, except treason, felony and breach of the peace, be privileged from arrest during their attendance at the session of their respective Houses, and in going to and returning from the same; and for any speech or debate in either House, they shall not be questioned in any other place.

No Senator or Representative shall, during the time for which he was elected, be appointed to any civil office under the authority of the United States, which shall have been created, or the emoluments whereof shall have been increased during such time: and no person holding any office under the United States, shall be a member of either House during his continuance in office.

Section 7. All bills for raising revenue shall originate in the House of Representatives; but the Senate may propose or concur with amendments as on other Bills.

Every bill which shall have passed the House of Representatives and the Senate, shall, before it become a law, be presented to the President of the United States; if he approve he shall sign it, but if not he shall return it, with his objections to that House in which it shall have originated, who shall enter the objections at large on their journal, and proceed to reconsider it. If after such reconsideration two thirds of that House shall agree to pass the bill, it shall be sent, together with the objections, to the other House, by which it shall likewise be reconsidered, and if approved by two thirds of that House, it shall become a law. But in all such cases the votes of both Houses shall be determined by yeas and nays, and the names of the persons voting for and against the bill shall be entered on the journal of each House respectively. If any bill shall not be returned by the President within ten days (Sundays excepted) after it shall have been presented to him, the same shall be a law, in like manner as if he had signed it, unless the Congress by their adjournment prevent its return, in which case it shall not be a law.

Every order, resolution, or vote to which the concurrence of the Senate and House of Representatives may be necessary (except on a question of adjournment) shall be presented to the President of the United States; and before the same shall take effect, shall be approved by him, or being disapproved by him, shall be repassed by two thirds of the Senate and House of Representatives, according to the rules and limitations prescribed in the case of a bill.

Section 8. The Congress shall have power to lay and collect taxes, duties, imposts and excises, to pay the debts and provide for the common defense and general
Constitution of the United States continued...
welfare of the United States; but all duties, imposts and excises shall be uniform throughout the United States;

To borrow money on the credit of the United States;

Constitution of the United States continued...

To regulate commerce with foreign nations, and among the several states, and with the Indian tribes;

To establish a uniform rule of naturalization, and uniform laws on the subject of bankruptcies throughout the United States;
To coin money, regulate the value thereof, and of foreign coin, and fix the standard of weights and measures;

To provide for the punishment of counterfeiting the securities and current coin of the United States;

To establish post offices and post roads;

To promote the progress of science and useful arts, by securing for limited times to authors and inventors the exclusive right to their respective writings and discoveries;

To constitute tribunals inferior to the Supreme Court;

To define and punish piracies and felonies committed on the high seas, and offenses against the law of nations;

To declare war, grant letters of marque and reprisal, and make rules concerning captures on land and water;

To raise and support armies, but no appropriation of money to that use shall be for a longer term than two years;

To provide and maintain a navy;

To make rules for the government and regulation of the land and naval forces;

To provide for calling forth the militia to execute the laws of the union, suppress insurrections and repel invasions;

To provide for organizing, arming, and disciplining, the militia, and for governing such part of them as may be employed in the service of the United States, reserving to the states respectively, the appointment of the officers, and the authority of training the militia according to the discipline prescribed by Congress;

To exercise exclusive legislation in all cases whatsoever, over such District (not exceeding ten miles square) as may, by cession of particular states, and the acceptance of Congress, become the seat of the government of the United States, and to exercise like authority over all places purchased by the consent of the legislature of the state in which the same shall be, for the erection of forts, magazines, arsenals, dockyards, and other needful buildings;

Constitution of the United States continued...

To make all laws which shall be necessary and proper for carrying into execution the foregoing powers, and all other powers vested by this Constitution in the government of the United States, or in any department or officer thereof.

Section 9. The migration or importation of such persons as any of the states now existing shall think proper to admit, shall not be prohibited by the Congress prior to the year one thousand eight hundred and eight, but a tax or duty may be imposed on such importation, not exceeding ten dollars for each person.

The privilege of the writ of habeas corpus shall not be suspended, unless when in cases of rebellion or invasion the public safety may require it.

No bill of attainder or ex post facto Law shall be passed.

{No capitation, or other direct, tax shall be laid, unless in proportion to the census or enumeration herein before directed to be taken.[5]}

No tax or duty shall be laid on articles exported from any state.

No preference shall be given by any regulation of commerce or revenue to the ports of one state over those of another: nor shall vessels bound to, or from, one state, be obliged to enter, clear or pay duties in another.

No money shall be drawn from the treasury, but in consequence of appropriations made by law; and a regular statement and account of receipts and expenditures of all public money shall be published from time to time.

No title of nobility shall be granted by the United States: and no person holding any office of profit or trust under them, shall, without the consent of the Congress, accept of any present, emolument, office, or title, of any kind whatever, from any king, prince, or foreign state.

Section 10. No state shall enter into any treaty, alliance, or confederation; grant letters of marque and reprisal; coin money; emit bills of credit; make anything but gold and silver coin a tender in payment of debts; pass any bill of attainder, ex post facto law, or law impairing the obligation of contracts, or grant any title of nobility.

No state shall, without the consent of the Congress, lay any imposts or duties on imports or exports, except what may be absolutely necessary for executing it's inspection laws: and the net produce of all duties and imposts, laid by any state on imports or exports, shall be for the use of the treasury of the United States; and all such laws shall be subject to the revision and control of the Congress.

No state shall, without the consent of Congress, lay any duty of tonnage, keep troops, or ships of war in time of peace, enter into any agreement or compact with another state, or with a foreign power, or engage in war, unless actually invaded, or in such imminent danger as will not admit of delay.

Constitution of the United States continued...

Article II

Section 1. The executive power shall be vested in a President of the United States of America. He shall hold his office during the term of four years {6}, and, together with the Vice President, chosen for the same term, be elected, as follows:

Each state shall appoint, in such manner as the Legislature thereof may direct, a number of electors, equal to the whole number of Senators and Representatives to which the State may be entitled in the Congress: but no Senator or Representative, or person holding an office of trust or profit under the United States, shall be appointed an elector.

{The electors shall meet in their respective states, and vote by ballot for two persons, of whom one at least shall not be an inhabitant of the same state with themselves. And they shall make a list of all the persons voted for, and of the number of votes for each; which list they shall sign and certify, and transmit sealed to the seat of the government of the United States, directed to the President of the Senate. The President of the Senate shall, in the presence of the Senate and House of Representatives, open all the certificates, and the votes shall then be counted. The person having the greatest number of votes shall be the President, if such number be a majority of the whole number of electors appointed; and if there be more than one who have such majority, and have an equal number of votes, then the House of Representatives shall immediately choose by ballot one of them for President; and if no person have a majority, then from the five highest on the list the said House shall in like manner choose the President. But in choosing the President, the votes shall be taken by States, the representation from each state having one vote; A quorum for this purpose shall consist of a member or members from two thirds of the states, and a majority of all the states shall be necessary to a choice. In every case, after the choice of the President, the person having the greatest number of votes of the electors shall be the Vice President. But if there should remain two or more who have equal votes, the Senate shall choose from them by ballot the Vice President.[7]}

The Congress may determine the time of choosing the electors, and the day on which they shall give their votes; which day shall be the same throughout the United States.

No person except a natural born citizen, or a citizen of the United States, at the time of the adoption of this Constitution, shall be eligible to the office of President; neither shall any person be eligible to that office who shall not have attained to the age of thirty five years, and been fourteen Years a resident within the United States.

{In case of the removal of the President from office, or of his death, resignation, or inability to discharge the powers and duties of the said office, the same shall devolve on the Vice President, and the Congress may by law provide for the case of removal, death, resignation or inability, both of the President and Vice President, declaring what officer shall then act as President, and such officer shall act accordingly, until the disability be removed, or a President shall be elected.[8]}

The President shall, at stated times, receive for his services, a compensation, which shall neither be increased nor diminished during the period for which he shall have been elected, and he shall not receive within that period any other emolument from the United States, or any of them.

Before he enter on the execution of his office, he shall take the following oath or affirmation: — "I do solemnly swear (or affirm) that I will faithfully execute the office of President of the United States, and will to the best of my ability, preserve, protect and defend the Constitution of the United States."

Section 2. The President shall be commander in chief of the Army and Navy of the United States, and of the militia of the several states, when called into the actual service of the United States; he may require the opinion, in writing, of the principal officer in each of the executive departments, upon any subject relating to the duties of their respective offices, and he shall have power to grant reprieves and pardons for offenses against the United States, except in cases of impeachment.

He shall have power, by and with the advice and consent of the Senate, to make treaties, provided two thirds of the Senators present concur; and he shall nominate, and by and with the advice and consent of the Senate, shall appoint ambassadors, other public ministers and consuls, judges of the Supreme Court, and all other officers of the United States, whose appointments are not herein otherwise provided for, and which shall be established by law: but the Congress may by law vest the appointment of such inferior officers, as they think proper, in the President alone, in the courts of law, or in the heads of departments.

The President shall have power to fill up all vacancies that may happen during the recess of the Senate, by granting commissions which shall expire at the end of their next session.

Section 3. He shall from time to time give to the Congress information of the state of the union, and recommend to their consideration such measures as he shall judge necessary and expedient; he may, on extraordinary occasions, convene both Houses, or either of them, and in case of disagreement between them, with respect to the time of adjournment, he may adjourn them to such time as he shall think proper; he shall receive ambassadors and other public ministers; he shall take care that the laws be faithfully executed, and shall commission all the officers of the United States.

Section 4. The President, Vice President and all civil officers of the United States, shall be removed from office on impeachment for, and conviction of, treason, bribery, or other high crimes and misdemeanors.

Article III

Constitution of the United States continued...

Section 1. The judicial power of the United States, shall be vested in one Supreme Court, and in such inferior courts as the Congress may from time to time ordain and establish. The judges, both of the supreme and inferior courts, shall hold their offices during good behaviour, and shall, at stated times, receive for their services, a compensation, which shall not be diminished during their continuance in office.

Section 2. The judicial power shall extend to all cases, in law and equity, arising under this Constitution, the laws of the United States, and treaties made, or which shall be made, under their authority; — to all cases affecting ambassadors, other public ministers and consuls; — to all cases of admiralty and maritime jurisdiction; — to controversies to which the United States shall be a party; — to controversies between two or more states; — {**between a state and citizens of another state**[9]}; — between citizens of different states; — between citizens of the same state claiming lands under grants of different states, and between a state, or the citizens thereof, and foreign states, citizens or subjects.

In all cases affecting ambassadors, other public ministers and consuls, and those in which a state shall be party, the Supreme Court shall have original jurisdiction. In all the other cases before mentioned, the Supreme Court shall have appellate jurisdiction, both as to law and fact, with such exceptions, and under such regulations as the Congress shall make.

The trial of all crimes, except in cases of impeachment, shall be by jury; and such trial shall be held in the state where the said crimes shall have been committed; but when not committed within any state, the trial shall be at such place or places as the Congress may by law have directed.

Section 3. Treason against the United States, shall consist only in levying war against them, or in adhering to their enemies, giving them aid and comfort. No person shall be convicted of treason unless on the testimony of two witnesses to the same overt act, or on confession in open court.

The Congress shall have power to declare the punishment of treason, but no attainder of treason shall work corruption of blood, or forfeiture except during the life of the person attainted.

Article IV

Section 1. Full faith and credit shall be given in each state to the public acts, records, and judicial proceedings of every other state. And the Congress may by general laws prescribe the manner in which such acts, records, and proceedings shall be proved, and the effect thereof.

Section 2. The citizens of each state shall be entitled to all privileges and immunities of citizens in the several states.

A person charged in any state with treason, felony, or other crime, who shall flee from justice, and be found in another state, shall on demand of the executive authority of the state from which he fled, be delivered up, to be removed to the state having jurisdiction of the crime.

{**No person held to service or labor in one state, under the laws thereof, escaping into another, shall, in consequence of any law or regulation therein, be discharged from such service or labor, but shall be delivered up on claim of the party to whom such service or labor may be due.**[10]}

Section 3. New states may be admitted by the Congress into this union; but no new states shall be formed or erected within the jurisdiction of any other state; nor any state be formed by the junction of two or more states, or parts of states, without the consent of the legislatures of the states concerned as well as of the Congress.

The Congress shall have power to dispose of and make all needful rules and regulations respecting the territory or other property belonging to the United States; and nothing in this Constitution shall be so construed as to prejudice any claims of the United States, or of any particular state.

Section 4. The United States shall guarantee to every state in this union a republican form of government, and shall protect each of them against invasion; and on application of the legislature, or of the executive (when the legislature cannot be convened) against domestic violence.

Article V

The Congress, whenever two thirds of both houses shall deem it necessary, shall propose amendments to this Constitution, or, on the application of the legislatures of two thirds of the several states, shall call a convention for proposing amendments, which, in either case, shall be valid to all intents and purposes, as part of this Constitution, when ratified by the legislatures of three fourths of the several states, or by conventions in three fourths thereof, as the one or the other mode of ratification may be proposed by the Congress; provided that no amendment which may be made prior to the year one thousand eight hundred and eight shall in any manner affect the first and fourth clauses in the ninth section of the first article; and that no state, without its consent, shall be deprived of its equal suffrage in the Senate.

Article VI

All debts contracted and engagements entered into, before the adoption of this Constitution, shall be as valid against the United States under this Constitution, as under the Confederation.

This Constitution, and the laws of the United States which shall be made in pursuance thereof; and all treaties made, or which shall be made, under the authority of the United States, shall be the supreme law of the land; and the judges in every state shall be bound thereby, anything in the Constitution or laws of any State to the contrary notwithstanding.

Constitution of the United States continued...

The Senators and Representatives before mentioned, and the members of the several state legislatures, and all executive and judicial officers, both of the United States and of the several states, shall be bound by oath or affirmation, to support this Constitution; but no religious test shall ever be required as a qualification to any office or public trust under the United States.

Article VII

The ratification of the conventions of nine states, shall be sufficient for the establishment of this Constitution between the states so ratifying the same.

Done in convention by the unanimous consent of the states present the seventeenth day of September in the year of our Lord one thousand seven hundred and eighty seven and of the independence of the United States of America the twelfth.

Footnotes

1   *Changed by Section 2 of the Fourteenth Amendment*
2   *Changed by the Seventeenth Amendment*
3   *Changed by the Seventeenth Amendment*
4   *Changed by Section 2 of the Twentieth Amendment*
5   *See Sixteenth Amendment*
6   *Limited to two terms by the Twenty-Second Amendment*
7   *Changed by the Twelfth Amendment*
8   *Changed by the Twenty-Fifth Amendment*
9   *Changed by the Eleventh Amendment*
10   *Changed by the Thirteenth Amendment*

Original Ten Amendments: The Bill of Rights

Passed by Congress September 25, 1789
Ratified December 15, 1791

Amendment I

Freedoms, Petitions, Assembly

Congress shall make no law respecting an establishment of religion, or prohibiting the free exercise thereof; or abridging the freedom of speech, or of the press, or the right of the people peaceably to assemble, and to petition the Government for a redress of grievances.

Amendment II

Right to bear arms

A well regulated Militia, being necessary to the security of a free State, the right of the people to keep and bear Arms, shall not be infringed.

Amendment III

Quartering of soldiers

No Soldier shall, in time of peace be quartered in any house, without the consent of the Owner, nor in time of war, but in a manner to be prescribed by law.

Amendment IV

Search and arrest

The right of the people to be secure in their persons, houses, papers, and effects, against unreasonable searches and seizures, shall not be violated, and no Warrants shall issue, but upon probable cause, supported by Oath or affirmation, and particularly describing the place to be searched, and the persons or things to be seized.

Amendment V

Rights in criminal cases

No person shall be held to answer for a capital, or otherwise infamous crime, unless on a presentment or indictment of a Grand Jury, except in cases arising in the land or naval forces, or in the Militia, when in actual service in time of War or public danger; nor shall any person be subject for the same offence to be twice put in jeopardy of life or limb, nor shall be compelled in any criminal case to be a witness against himself, nor be deprived of life, liberty, or property, without due process of law; nor shall private property be taken for public use, without just compensation.

Amendment VI

Right to a fair trial

In all criminal prosecutions, the accused shall enjoy the right to a speedy and public trial, by an impartial jury of the State and district wherein the crime shall have been committed; which district shall have been previously ascertained by law, and to be informed of the nature and cause of the accusation; to be confronted with the witnesses against him; to have compulsory process for obtaining witnesses in his favor, and to have the assistance of counsel for his defense.

Amendment VII
Rights in civil cases
In Suits at common law, where the value in controversy shall exceed twenty dollars, the right of trial by jury shall be preserved, and no fact tried by a jury shall be otherwise re-examined in any Court of the United States, than according to the rules of the common law.

Amendment VIII
Bail, fines, punishment
Excessive bail shall not be required, nor excessive fines imposed, nor cruel and unusual punishments inflicted.

Amendment IX
Rights retained by the People
The enumeration in the Constitution of certain rights shall not be construed to deny or disparage others retained by the people.

Amendment X
States' rights
The powers not delegated to the United States by the Constitution, nor prohibited by it to the States, are reserved to the States respectively, or to the people.

Later Amendments

Amendment 11
Lawsuits against states
 The Judicial power of the United States shall not be construed to extend to any suit in law or equity, commenced or prosecuted against one of the United States by Citizens of another State, or by Citizens or Subjects of any Foreign State. February 7, 1795.

Amendment 12
Presidential elections

The Electors shall meet in their respective states, and vote by ballot for President and Vice-President, one of whom, at least, shall not be an inhabitant of the same state with themselves; they shall name in their ballots the person voted for as President, and in distinct ballots the person voted for as Vice-President, and they shall make distinct lists of all persons voted for as President, and of all persons voted for as Vice-President, and of the number of votes for each, which lists they shall sign and certify, and transmit sealed to the seat of the government of the United States, directed to the President of the Senate;--The President of the Senate shall, in the presence of the Senate and House of Representatives, open all the certificates and the votes shall then be counted;--The person having the greatest number of votes for President, shall be the President, if such number be a majority of the whole number of Electors appointed; and if no person have such majority, then from the persons having the highest numbers not exceeding three on the list of those voted for as President, the House of Representatives shall choose immediately, by ballot, the President. But in choosing the President, the votes shall be taken by states, the representation from each state having one vote; a quorum for this purpose shall consist of a member or members from two-thirds of the states, and a majority of all the states shall be necessary to a choice. [And if the House of Representatives shall not choose a President whenever the right of choice shall devolve upon them, before the fourth day of March next following, then the Vice-President shall act as President, as in the case of the death or other constitutional disability of the President.]* The person having the greatest number of votes as Vice-President, shall be the Vice-President, if such number be a majority of the whole number of Electors appointed, and if no person have a majority, then from the two highest numbers on the list, the Senate shall choose the Vice-President; a quorum for the purpose shall consist of two-thirds of the whole number of Senators, and a majority of the whole number shall be necessary to a choice. But no person constitutionally ineligible to the office of President shall be eligible to that of Vice-President of the United States. June 15, 1804. Superseded by Section 3 of the Twentieth Amendment.

Amendment 13
Abolition of slavery
Section 1. Neither slavery nor involuntary servitude, except as a punishment for crime whereof the party shall have been duly convicted, shall exist within the United States, or any place subject to their jurisdiction.
Section 2. Congress shall have power to enforce these articles by appropriate legislation. December 6, 1865.

Amendment 14
Civil rights

Section 1. All persons born or naturalized in the United States and subject to the jurisdiction thereof, are citizens of the United States and of the State wherein they reside. No State shall make or enforce any law which shall abridge the privileges or immunities of citizens of the United States; nor shall any State deprive any person of life, liberty, or property, without due process of law; nor deny to any person within its jurisdiction the equal protection of the laws.

Section 2. Representatives shall be apportioned among the several States according to their respective numbers, counting the whole number of persons in each State, excluding Indians not taxed. But when the right to vote at any election for the choice of electors for President and Vice President of the United States, Representatives in Congress, the Executive and Judicial officers of a State, or the members of the Legislature thereof, is denied to any of the male inhabitants of such State, being twenty-one years of age, and citizens of the United States, or in any way abridged, except for participation in rebellion, or other crime, the basis of representation therein shall be reduced in the proportion which the number of such male citizens shall bear to the whole number of male citizens twenty-one years of age in such State.

Section 3. No person shall be a Senator or Representative in Congress, or elector of President and Vice President, or hold any office, civil or military, under the United States, or under any State, who, having previously taken an oath, as a member of Congress, or as an officer of the United States, or as a member of any State legislature, or as an executive or judicial officer of any State, to support the Constitution of the United States, shall have engaged in insurrection or rebellion against the same, or given aid or comfort to the enemies thereof. But Congress may by a vote of two-thirds of each House, remove such disability.

Section 4. The validity of the public debt of the United States, authorized by law, including debts incurred for payment of pensions and bounties for services in suppressing insurrection or rebellion, shall not be questioned. But neither the United States nor any State shall assume or pay any debt or obligation incurred in aid of insurrection or rebellion against the United States, or any claim for the loss or emancipation of any slave; but all such debts, obligations and claims shall be held illegal and void.

Section 5. The Congress shall have power to enforce, by appropriate legislation, the provisions of this article. July 9, 1868.

Amendment 15
Black suffrage
Section 1. The right of citizens of the United States to vote shall not be denied or abridged by the United States or by any State on account of race, color, or previous condition of servitude.

Section 2. The Congress shall have power to enforce this article by appropriate legislation. February 3, 1870.

Amendment 16
Income taxes

The Congress shall have power to lay and collect taxes on incomes, from whatever source derived, without apportionment among the several States, and without regard to any census or enumeration. February 3, 1913.

Amendment 17
Senatorial elections

The Senate of the United States shall be composed of two senators from each State, elected by the people thereof, for six years; and each Senator shall have one vote. The electors in each State shall have the qualifications requisite for electors of the most numerous branch of the State legislature. When vacancies happen in the representation of any State in the Senate, the executive authority of such State shall issue writs of election to fill such vacancies: Provided, That the legislature of any State may empower the executive thereof to make temporary appointments until the people fill the vacancies by election as the legislature may direct. This amendment shall not be so construed as to affect the election or term of any Senator chosen before it becomes valid as part of the Constitution. April 8, 1913.

Amendment 18
Prohibition of liquor

Section 1. After one year from the ratification of this article, the manufacture, sale, or transportation of intoxicating liquors within, the importation thereof into, or the exportation thereof from the United States and all territory subject to the jurisdiction thereof for beverage purposes is hereby prohibited.

Section 2. The Congress and the several States shall have concurrent power to enforce this article by appropriate legislation.

Section 3. This article shall be inoperative unless it shall have been ratified as an amendment to the Constitution by the legislatures of the several States, as provided in the Constitution, within seven years from the date of the submission hereof to the States by the Congress. January 16, 1919. Repealed by the Twenty-First, December 5, 1933.

Amendment 19
Women's suffrage

The Bill of Rights continued...

The right of citizens of the United States to vote shall not be denied or abridged by the United States or by any States on account of sex. Congress shall have power to enforce this article by appropriate legislation. August 18, 1920.

Amendment 20
Terms of office

Section 1. The terms of the President and Vice President shall end at noon the 20th day of January, and the terms of Senators and Representatives at noon on the 3d day of January, of the years in which such terms would have ended if this article had not been ratified; and the terms of their successors shall then begin.

Section 2. The Congress shall assemble at least once in every year, and such meeting shall begin at noon on the 3d day of January, unless they shall by law appoint a different day.

Section 3. If, at the time fixed for the beginning of the term of the President, the President elect shall have died, the Vice President elect shall become President. If a President shall not have been chosen before the time fixed for the beginning of his term, or if the President elect shall have failed to qualify, then the Vice President elect shall act as President until a President shall have qualified; and the Congress may by law provide for the case wherein neither a President elect nor a Vice President elect shall have qualified, declaring who shall then act as President, or the manner in which one who is to act shall be selected, and such person shall act accordingly until a President or Vice President shall have qualified.

Section 4. The Congress may by law provide for the case of the death of any of the persons from whom the House of Representatives may choose a President whenever the right of choice shall have devolved upon them, and for the case of the death of any of the persons from whom the Senate may choose a Vice President whenever the right of choice shall have devolved upon them.

Section 5. Sections 1 and 2 shall take effect on the 15th day of October following the ratification of this article.

Section 6. This article shall be inoperative unless it shall have been ratified as an amendment to the Constitution by the legislatures of three-fourths of the several States within seven years from the date of its submission. January 23, 1933.

Amendment 21
Repeal of Prohibition

Section 1. The eighteenth article of amendment to the Constitution of the United States is hereby repealed.

Section 2. The transportation or importation into any State, Territory, or possession of the United States for delivery or use therein of intoxicating liquors, in violation of the laws thereof, is hereby prohibited.

Section 3. The article shall be inoperative unless it shall have been ratified as an amendment to the Constitution by conventions in the several States, as provided in the Constitution, within seven years from the date of the submission hereof to the States by the Congress. December 5, 1933.

Amendment 22
Term Limits for the Presidency

Section 1. No person shall be elected to the office of the President more than twice, and no person who has held the office of President, or acted as President, for more than two years of a term to which some other person was elected President shall be elected to the office of the President more than once. But this Article shall not apply to any person holding the office of President when this Article was proposed by the Congress, and shall not prevent any person who may be holding the office of President, or acting as President, during the term within which this Article becomes operative from holding the office of President or acting as President during the remainder of such term.

Section 2. This article shall be inoperative unless it shall have been ratified as an amendment to the Constitution by the legislatures of three-fourths of the several States within seven years from the date of its submission to the States by the Congress. February 27, 1951.

Amendment 23
Washington, D.C., suffrage

Section 1. The District constituting the seat of government of the United States shall appoint in such manner as the Congress may direct: A number of electors of President and Vice President equal to the whole number of Senators and Representatives in Congress to which the District would be entitled if it were a state, but in no event more than the least populous State; they shall be in addition to those appointed by the States, but they shall be considered, for the purposes of the election of President and Vice President, to be electors appointed by a State; and they shall meet in the District and perform such duties as provided by the twelfth article of amendment.

Section 2. The Congress shall have power to enforce this article by appropriate legislation. March 29, 1961.

Amendment 24
Abolition of poll taxes

The Bill of Rights continued...

Section 1. The right of citizens of the United States to vote in any primary or other election for President or Vice President, for electors for President or Vice President, or for Senator or Representative in Congress, shall not be denied or abridged by the United States or any State by reason of failure to pay any poll tax or other tax.

Section 2. The Congress shall have power to enforce this article by appropriate legislation. January 23, 1964.

Amendment 25
Presidential succession

Section 1. In case of the removal of the President from office or of his death or resignation, the Vice President shall become President.

Section 2. Whenever there is a vacancy in the office of the Vice President, the President shall nominate a Vice President who shall take office upon confirmation by a majority vote of both Houses of Congress.

Section 3. Whenever the President transmits to the President pro tempore of the Senate and the Speaker of the House of Representatives his written declaration that he is unable to discharge the powers and duties of his office, and until he transmits to them a written declaration to the contrary, such powers and duties shall be discharged by the Vice President as Acting President.

Section 4. Whenever the Vice President and a majority of either the principal officers of the executive departments or of such other body as Congress may by law provide, transmit to the President pro tempore of the Senate and the Speaker of the House of Representatives their written declaration that the President is unable to discharge the powers and duties of his office, the Vice President shall immediately assume the powers and duties of the office as Acting President. Thereafter, when the President transmits to the President pro tempore of the Senate and the Speaker of the House of Representatives his written declaration that no inability exists, he shall resume the powers and duties of his office unless the Vice President and a majority of either the principal officers of the executive department or of such other body as Congress may by law provide, transmit within four days to the President pro tempore of the Senate and the Speaker of the House of Representatives their written declaration that the President is unable to discharge the powers and duties of his office. Thereupon Congress shall decide the issue, assembling within forty-eight hours for that purpose if not in session. If the Congress, within twenty-one days after receipt of the latter written declaration, or, if Congress is not in session, within twenty-one days after Congress is required to assemble, determines by two-thirds vote of both Houses that the President is unable to discharge the powers and duties of his office, the Vice President shall continue to discharge the same as Acting President; otherwise, the President shall resume the powers and duties of his office. February 10, 1967.

Amendment 26
18-year-old suffrage
Section 1. The right of citizens of the United States, who are eighteen years of age or older, to vote shall not be denied or abridged by the United States or by any State on account of age.
Section 2. The Congress shall have power to enforce this article by appropriate legislation. June 30, 1971.

Amendment 27
Congressional pay raises
No law, varying the compensation for the services of the Senators and Representatives, shall take effect, until an election of Representatives shall have intervened. May 7, 1992. (Note: Congress submitted the text of this amendment as part of the proposed Bill of Rights on September 27, 1789. The Amendment was not ratified together with the first ten Amendments.)